"An older adult writes   he
heartfelt words into typed text. It's a beautiful partnership across time.

The words of these stories bring back the past, but more important
than that, they fulfill our common human need to be heard, to be
listened to, to connect. This inspired program, represented so movingly
in this storybook, provides a safe environment for older adults to tell
their stories, and the benefits are myriad. Knowing that their memories
will live forever means so much to the older participants, and we've
seen them flourish as a result; and for the young adult scribes, every
session is an opportunity that teaches about giving and sharing and
connecting, and how being of service is enriching on so many levels.

Long live the words of these Best Day stories, and may the voices
represented know that someone out there is listening."

- Lisa Marsh Ryerson, AARP Foundation President

Dear Deborah,
It was a pleasure
to meet you today!
Happy story listening :)
- Benita

About *The Best Day of My Life So Far*

The Best Day of My Life So Far is a registered 501(c)(3) non-profit organization. Inspired by her friendship with her grandmother, architect Benita Cooper founded our organization in 2009 with a single group in Philadelphia, and a blog – to empower seniors and engage younger people through storytelling.

Now, our signature storytelling groups and blogs are spreading across the country. Our methods have been researched and evaluated by international research teams and featured in numerous media outlets, academic journals, and professional conferences. AARP is among our program partners.

Meet our senior storytellers nationwide and hear their inspiring stories at www.bestdayofmylifesofar.org. Like us on Facebook (The Best Day of My Life So Far), follow us on Twitter (@bestdaysofar) and join our Story Letter mailing list to be the first to see new stories as they are written. Donate to help us grow more groups and share more stories with you: P.O. Box 22458, Philadelphia PA 19110.

Inquiries should be directed to:
Best Day of My Life So Far, Inc.
info@bestdayofmylifesofar.org
www.bestdayofmylifesofar.org
PO Box 22458
Philadelphia PA 19110

Compilation © 2014 Best Day of My Life So Far, Inc.
Stories © 2014 As noted in the heading of each story

First Published in 2014 by Lulu Press
ISBN: 978-1-312-15177-2

Storybook Production Credits:
Benita Cooper, Founder and Executive Director
Andy Kahan and Thelma Reese, Editors
Jen Ross and Madi Garvin, Associate Editors
Caitlin Cieri, Editorial Assistant
Michelle Sheffer, Consulting Copy Editor
Book Design by: Alex Visconti

The Best Day of My Life So Far

Stories to give you courage
through the good times and the bad

Editors
Andy Kahan and Thelma Reese

Editorial Team
Emily Antoszyk, Caitlin Cieri, Madi Garvin, Jen Ross, and Michelle Sheffer

Designer
Alexandra Visconti

Founder
Benita Cooper

Original Best Day Senior Storytellers
2009–2013

Adel Mena

Aileen Jefferson

Amy Henson

Andrew Micheletti

Arlin Gordon

Arthur Murray

Barbara Giles

Barbara Moore

Beatrice Newkirk

Bernice Moore

Betty Hennigan

Brenda Bailey

Brenda Jones

Brenda Scantlebury

Bri Kurmue

Carmella Martino

Carol Dailey

Clementine Nix

Delores Slaughter

Doris Lang

Dorothy Gross

Dorothy Taylor

Edward McKinney

Edward McRumey

Elizabeth Byod

Elizabeth Cason

Elizabeth McCorkle

Elliot Doomes

Ellis Zelmanoff

Ernestyne Whiteside Bush

Evelyn Ward

Geraldine Gaskins

Gloria Bachlor

Greta Adams

Gwendolyn Jordan

Hattie Lee Ellerbe

Hazel Nurse

Helen Burnett

Helen H. Lahr

Henrietta Faust

Isadora Fields

Jan Michener

Jane A. Boyd

Jean McCallum

Jenny Gogo Williams

Jimmy Cary

Joann Bailey

Joan Bunting

Joann Fleming

Joan Frankenstein

John Keels

John Maloney

John Martino

Joseph Garrison

Josie Miller

Joyce D. Santos

Kathleen Herbert

Linda Bojazi

Linda Carr

Lisa Leung

Loretta Gaither

Louella Coplon

Luis Fuentes

Luvenia Black

Marci Zelmanoff

Marie Ricciuti

Mary Angelucci

Mary Minor

Mary-em Bristow

Maryann Wallace

Mattie McCall

Michael (Man-Tin)
    Chan

Millie Lilly

Missouri Grier

Mo McCooper

Mozell Roberts

Nancy Blair

Nancy Marie Wilson

Naomi Williamson

Norman Cain

Patricia Tucker

Patricia Williams

Paul Flint

Ramona Mapp

Richard Holley

Ridith Moore

Robert Hankins

Robert Leung

Robert Mitchell

Rochelle Tynes

Rongwen Zhang

Rosalind Smith

Rosires M. Raff

Santos Ruiz

Teresa Shue

Theo Newman

Theresa Son Lee

Thomas (Teddy) Coyle

Vernelle Lyles

Vicki Tate

William McDevitt

To Mei Hing Chiu – our founder's amazing "Po Po" whose stories and friendship inspired our mission

Contents

Introduction

On an otherwise ordinary summer day in 2006, I called my grandma for the first time ever in my life, just to talk. She was 85; I was 25. She was born in a Chinese village; I was born in the United States. She was living in a Seattle suburb; I was a young architect living in downtown Philadelphia. We had nothing in common – or so I thought. I thought we would run out of things to say after a few minutes of talking about the weather. Instead, we haven't stopped talking since.

The friendship and happiness that my grandma has given me through stories is so powerful that I have to share it. In September 2009, I started a storytelling class at a borrowed office in the basement of Philadelphia Senior Center and a blog – the class, to have a fun and supportive environment for seniors to open up through stories; the blog, to transport the seniors' voices beyond the confines of those basement walls to the ears of younger people near and far. The class was intended as a six-week workshop. It has been meeting every week, rain or shine, ever since.

Within months of the group's founding, people around the world asked to start groups of their own. In 2010, we began running test groups in diverse venues as far away as Hong Kong. In 2011, we built a model satellite in partnership with AARP and the Free Library of Philadelphia. In 2014, through an official Facilitator Training Guide, we launched a compact, flexible structure that allows anyone to start a group anywhere.

To date, our seniors have written thousands of stories in just our original group – and the number of stories multiplies with every new group. This book cannot contain our seniors' every word, but we hope that the diversity of their voices and the unity of their positive Best Day of My Life So Far spirit shows through.

The stories contained in the following pages are selected by an all-volunteer editorial team with ages ranging from 18 to 80, from the stories our seniors wrote in the first four years of our original group. These stories tell us not to give up. As seniors open up about facing or overcoming past or present struggles, we hope that this book reminds us all that the struggles we face are often similar to what older generations have experienced or conquered.

Proceeds from book sales will go towards growing more groups around the country and building an online library to preserve and share their stories.

Thank you for reading. And thank you for your support.

All My Best,

Benita Cooper
Founder and Executive Director
The Best Day of My Life So Far

Acknowledgments

This book would not be possible without the collaboration and support of the following people:

Our tireless all-volunteer storybook production team who took this book from concept, editing, to design;

Our greater Best Day of My Life So Far volunteer team who is working hard to nurture groups to start around the country, while nurturing our original group to thrive – I'd especially like to shine the spotlight on our humble, wonderful copy editors who have typed every story that every senior has ever written every single week;

Professionals who have offered us invaluable wisdom and services including our legal team at White and Williams and our consulting publisher The Head & The Hand Press;

Our longtime supporter AARP, who has publicly endorsed our work since our early days, and given us motivation and guidance every step of the way to scale to the national level;

AARP Foundation President, Lisa Marsh Ryerson, for her powerful opening testimonial;

Our blog readers, social media fans, event audience members – your listening ear is what keeps our seniors writing;

Every senior who has ever sat at a Best Day of My Life So Far table, and opened up through a personal story.

1

Arts

HIS MASTER'S VOICE

by Mo McCooper

The first records I ever heard were played on a turntable. They went around on top of a piece of wooden furniture called a Victrola at my grandmother's row house on Stanton St. in the East Falls neighborhood of Philadelphia, PA. The large records, as I recall, were almost as big as a round kitchen or office clock today.

"Don't You Believe It!" My favorites were recorded during the World War I years and were titled "Don't You Believe It!" and "She Lived Next Door to the Firehouse." They were funny songs, and all my cousins loved them. The record player had a handle on the side, which we took turns winding so that the music would keep playing.

In the middle of the large records were pictures of a dog with his head cocked so that one ear was in line with the music coming out of the original phonograph from the RCA Victor manufacturing plant in Camden, New Jersey. The title of the picture is "His Master's Voice."

Thanks, Grammom!

A GREAT FILM

by Hazel Nurse

According to one author, after the D.A.R. (Daughters of the American Revolution) denied Marian Anderson a performance saying that her race was the reason, Eleanor Roosevelt, wife of the President, resigned from the organization. Later, Mrs. Roosevelt influenced the formation of a black pilot training program at Tuskegee Institute in 1941.

It was gratifying to see the movie *Red Tails*, but even more so to see George Lucas finally producing the million-dollar investment after twenty-three years.

This further reinforced the fact that African American or black pilots had the intelligence, confidence, and expertise to be pilots.

BLUE SKIES

by Bernice Moore

"Stormy Weather," sung by Lena Horn, James Brown, and Frank Sinatra. "Blue Skies," *South Pacific*, and war songs. Night and day they had song-and-war movies. Nat King Cole, Dean Martin, and Doris Day were all good singers who sang some country music as well.

I went to the movies and had popcorn, candy, soda, and ice cream. But my favorite was the peanuts.
Going to the movies was fun, but coming out of the movies there were always people starting something.

But we always kept up with the new movies that were coming out, like Tarzan and Jane. Most of all the kids' movies and the funnies.

"Today there are still good people"

Everything was peaceful. Everyone had fun and had a smile on their face.

Today there are still good people. I like to see smiling faces whether old or young.

TIN PAN ALLEY

by Joe Garrison

This is about the time I went to New York City to the Brill Building. There were a lot of popular songs written there. I had a friend who worked at the center where I was working at: the Bucks County Center for the Blind. He had this idea that I could drum because I used to play at school when I was young. The Beatles were just breaking up in the 1970s, but my friend would bring in his Beatles records and have me play to the songs. Then he took me to the Brill Building to one of the rooms with a drum set and a radio, and I was to play to whatever was playing on the radio to a small audience. I thought I was pretty good, but I knew I wasn't as good as some of the people on the records. I must have played for half an hour to an hour.

Turns out I wasn't as good as I thought—at least according to them. They were professional judges. You think you're talented, and then you find out you are not as talented as you want to be; that's disappointing. I never played drums seriously afterwards, only for a hobby. I like singing better anyway, so I did more singing.

"I still like rock n' roll a lot"

I still like rock n' roll a lot—the music of the '60s and '70s. I love the Beatles, the Moody Blues, and Bob Dylan.

I also like Motown. I was glad I got to go to New York City and be in that famous building, even though I got a rude awakening, I didn't feel bad about the experience. It was back in my late 20s.

"Tin Pan Alley" was the nickname given to the Brill Building. It got the name because of where it was located, maybe because there were beggars walking around banging on tin pans. A lot of popular songs were written there in the 1930s and '40s. It is still famous for the sound that came out of its halls.

People Don't Write Songs Like that Any More

by Joe Garrison

I've been enjoying music practically my whole life. I've heard many kinds of songs and funny lyrics, but nowadays, novelty songs have disappeared.

One of the most novel of novelty songs is something you hear in Westerns all the time. But no one gives a thought to the nonsense lyrics. The song is called "O Susanna."

"It rained all night the day I left, the weather it was dry. The sun so hot, I froze to death; Susanna, don't you cry."

Every form of music has its nonsense songs and lyrics, whether it's rhythm and blues (R&B) or country and western or sometimes even soul music. You are bound to find one song that's purely fun.

In 1950, there was a famous R&B singing group called The Coasters. They sang funny and clever songs such as "Charlie Brown" and '"Poison Ivy" and "Run Red Run."

But the funniest song title I remember was by Homer and Jethro: "I Got Tears In My Ears From Lying On My Back In My Bed While I Cry Over You."

"I miss the day of the nonsense and novelty songs"

Nowadays every song is so serious, and I miss the day of the nonsense and novelty songs. I hope that someday, someone will remember that life can still have funny moments. I hope the novelty and nonsense songs will come back.

Flying Dutchman and Lone Ranger

by Joe Garrison

To be a true music lover, you have to appreciate all forms of music, from the novelty songs to the symphony. All music can be fun or serious, and it can have different meanings to different people. What I'm saying is, you may like country

"all music can be fun or serious"

and western; someone else may like rock and roll or blues.

Opera may not be my favorite form of music, but I am familiar with a few famous arias.

I did listen to one complete opera and I enjoyed it. I really enjoyed it, actually. It was *The Flying Dutchman* by Richard Wagner. It only has one act, but it is a fantastic drama about a ghost ship.

I liked it because the overture is so familiar to me. It's exciting because it was used later as the background music for chase scenes in *The Lone Ranger*. That goes to show how opera music has its place now, still. It's timeless. I feel that way about music. Good music.

I can get the same enjoyment listening to the Beatles as I get from Beethoven.

THE BEAT OF THE DRUMS

by Joe Garrison

Back in the 1940s, there seemed to be a unique way of selling products on the radio. Big bands were still popular, and one of the features of the big bands was that the drummers would have a solo.

If you had a snappy jingle with a rhythm beat you could sell anything. In fact most of the jingles were for soap and laundry detergent. As commercials got sophisticated in the 1950s and '60s, you didn't hear anybody beating their drums to a snazzy rhythm anymore. Instead, you heard background piano music. Some commercials even imitated game shows and had little dramatic skits.

MOVIES

by Mo McCooper

The Saturday afternoon main movies were stuff like *Tarzan of the Apes* or one of the many other Tarzan movies. Johnny Weissmuller was our favorite of about half-a-dozen other actors who played the Apeman. He was an Olympic medal winner in swimming and

"Cheetah and the chimpanzee always pleased the crowd"

really looked the part. Cheetah the chimpanzee always pleased the crowd, and the crocodiles, snakes, and poisonous plants kept the danger level up. Tarzan's yell would echo all over Hungrytown after the movie house emptied out.

Gene Autry, Will Rodgers, Wild Bill Hickok, Red Ryder, Tom Mix, and Lash LaRue were some of the cowboy stars we cheered on. The Lone Ranger and Tonto were big, too. My favorite was Red Ryder. He didn't wear fancy clothes, and he took a little kid named Little Beaver on adventures with him.

2

Challenges

X-Mas Day 12.25.2010

by Henrietta Faust

He pretended to look at her striped dress.
He patted and said, "Is that real?" As only he patted her.
A touch from the gate of Hades!
This is one for the paper and ink.
But, how to put what a man did on paper?!
When the world and he say he didn't do it!
Example on TV – he pretended – one thing.
But what he did with his other hand
was criminal, offensive, and humiliating.
And, he pretended he had done nothing!
Please, stop this now!
This is for all who have been touched without their permission
And couldn't do one thing about it!
Destructive tyrants, abusers, and predators.
Destroying the innocence and peace with an unwanted touch.
Ruining a world by a touch.
Oh, I could put it on paper!?
But words can't explain when men do.
The Hades you feel now is what a man did!!

IT WILL COME TO PASS

by Loretta Gaither

I am still looking for housing. The place where I am right now is falling apart. I am working with the NAACP to get into a better place. The building where I am is dilapidated.

Everything is falling apart. There is mildew

"Everything is falling apart"

everywhere, ceilings are caving in, and ants are everywhere, the living situation is not right for us. I am going to continue to seek a new apartment.

When I come to the writing class it makes me feel better. I went to Bri's church, and another woman named Loretta helped me get home; she was very kind. These two things keep my mind together.

I am filling out applications for housing. I really appreciate the senior center because they give me a place to put my clothing. It is a beautiful thing when people do care. I consider many of the people at the church and shelter to be my family. I thank God and I keep praying that this stuff will pass.

When I water the plants in the center, that alone makes me feel better.

HOME AWAY FROM HOME

by Beatrice Newkirk

When my husband was away from home, I missed him very much. When he went away for the first three months, I thought three months was a long time. But the best time was when he returned home. Going to the movies and eating out at the restaurant was my favorite thing. Dressed in his uniform, he looked good. I always remember all the good times we had.

> *"I always remember all the good times"*

My sons, six of them, and a daughter went into the service. I had two sons in the Navy, and four sons in the Army. One daughter went into the Army. My husband went into the Marines. None of my sons wanted to go into the Marines. Every one is out of the service except one son. His name is Terry, and he is still in the Army.

Two of my sons were in Desert Storm. I am glad that I did not lose any of them.

Now I have two grandsons who want to go into the service, but I do not tell them not to go. It is up to them.

BATTLEFIELD FOR VETERANS

by Loretta Gaither

I talked to some veterans to come to the chapel and tell people their stories of how they fought on the front line. I asked several other people to come and hear these stories.

"tell people their stories"

It felt good to help the veterans feel better because they do not get enough recognition for fighting for our country. Veterans do not get enough benefits for fighting for our country, either—some have lost eyes, lost legs, lost friends. Some had to climb over dead bodies on the battlefield. It is unfair to them to not have benefits or a place to live instead of living on the streets. People look at them like they are nobody, but they have done a lot for our country and all of us. It is not right!

3

Culture

1947

by Amy Henson

I never really understood why I treasure a tattered, creased, many-times-folded-and-unfolded paper that

"I was born in Germany"

looks older than me. It is a record of birth that was issued at the village city hall; I was born in Germany. Funny thing is that I didn't live there very long.

I was born on the third story of a village house with a midwife attending. The house belonged to a family of German citizens. My mom and dad lived on the third floor of their home. After the war (the one they call "the big one"), the United States required German citizens to allow officers with families to use their homes. I understand that they actually told the Germans to leave their homes but my parents asked only for a room and were graciously accepted by this family.

I have another record of birth that is not as treasured. It used to make me cry, and it sometimes makes me sad. My dad was in the Army in Germany and found, fell in love with, and married a German girl. The US Army insisted that my dad bring my mother and myself to the Army hospital on base because, although I was already born and doing well, I was a U.S. citizen.

As my mom was being taken from the ambulance, my dad arrived to the area as we entered the hospital. Someone (mom never said who) approached us and told them to put us back into the ambulance and take us to the "black" hospital. You see, mom and dad outwardly had very different skin colors. There is more to this story that is hurtful, but these days have passed and that part is more my mom's story. A U.S. birth certificate was issued for me.

The birth record issued on behalf of the U.S. government reads female, born 5/5/1947, race MULATTO. The German record does not have a category for race. I do not feel that I am different from anyone else, although many have tried to make me feel and understand that I am (from another point of view).

Times have changed a lot, but to me it should have always been as my first birth record stated: female child born 5/5/1947.

"Times have changed"

LIFE

by Arlin Gordon

I'd like to talk about life because life is so interesting. I grew up in a family of eleven children. I was raised by my mother, father, and grandfather. One thing that was interesting about Grandpa was that he always checked our homework. He'd say, "This is right, this is not right." It wasn't 'til he had passed and we were talking years later that somebody said, "Grandpa couldn't read." And I said, "What? Say that again?" But, you know, it didn't matter that he couldn't read. He was always able to make us do our homework.

"Grandpa couldn't read"

THE LETTER

by Arlin Gordon

Riding the bus the other day I noticed a lot of people doing a lot of things. Some people were on their cell phones talking, some were texting. Some were complaining, and I began to wonder how we've lost the personal touch with one another. Nowadays when communicating with our loved ones, strangers, or friends, we are either texting, emailing, or sending faxes—we have Facebook and we're tweeting. We no longer take the time to write a letter. A letter tells someone that you care. There's so much joy in reading a letter that someone personally sends to you. Can you imagine how that person would feel

"There's so much joy in reading a letter"

to receive a personal letter from you? Where has the letter gone?

I AM FROM...

by Bri Kurume

1. I Am From: Rats and mice and from roaches and flies and chinches and nightmares.

2. I Am From: An overly crowded (2) bedroom house filled with (9) people, (1) dog, (1) cat and (1) toilet.

3. I Am From: The deliciously cooked pots of pigtails and smoked meat, collard greens, the yams, baked candied and sweet. The taste still lingers on my tongue and in the crevices of my mind.

4. I Am From: Bless your food before you eat. Wash your hands before you go into the refrig. Most definitely wash your hands after using the bathroom.

5. I Am From: Nettie-Mae Spurell Spivey. And she was the MOTHER. A strict disciplinarian. And she had a humorous personality. One of the best mommies that ever walked this earth. I will never forget her goodness, nor her love.

6a. I Am From: The place of horrid existence, struggled living and continuous love, thrift store shopping with a practiced eye, searching for the best and finest clothing for her (6) children, who were always the best dressed children in the neighborhood, public schools and Church.

6b. I Am From: Boys' hair cuts, girls' hair pressed/curled plus touched up every (2) weeks.

6c. From: Her Mantra. If you lie, you will steal. If you steal, you will take drugs and kill, then end up in the jail house. And: That we (my brother/sisters) should always remember and believe that Jesus loves you and holds you in the hollow of His hands.

7a. I Am From: A Christian background, Sunday school, Bible study, and Church all day Sunday.

7b. Having to renew my faith continuously as I journeyed thru this harried life.

8a. I Am From: Prejudiced North America, and I am an Afro-American female.

8b: (2) foods that represent family: Boxes of Argo starch and bottles of Pepsi Cola.

9a: From: Jimmy Martin. An absent father and a person whom we (brothers/sisters) never recognized as father and never called daddy! He was only a shadow in our lives. It took me many years to comprehend how my mom could even love* such a man, let alone have children by him.

* But life's journey has taught me about that emotion—love—and how it can color your best intentions and shade your dreams.

9b. From the: Wonderful, sweet, loving maternal grandmother that was always there for Nettie-Mae, and her (6) children, bringing food when the belly and the cupboard was empty. Buying us comic books, jump ropes, skates, and even a puppy for Xmas. She also took us to the seashore in the summer time. I was named after her.

10. I Am From: Nettie-Mae Spurell Spivey and Jimmy Martin. Each has since died and now uses Heaven as an address. Leaving on Planet Earth—Jimmy, Sandy, Cukie, Carl, and Rickey. The essence of their shared love.

"essence of their shared love"

PATTON STREET VILLAGE

by Hattie Lee Ellerbe

As a young married couple, my husband and I moved to the 1900 block of North Patton Street. We were among the first to integrate this block and were not very welcomed by our "other" neighbors.
It was October 1956 and we were in our early-to-mid-twenties and had one three-year-old daughter, Karen.

As the years went by, more young families had moved in, and by the mid 1960s, all of "the darker persuasion." There were many, many children, and everyone seemed happy and interested in each other's welfare.
Our children played together and went to school and in some cases went to church together.

Parents didn't just take their children on trips. They would ask permission and take some of the neighbor's children with them. It wasn't unusual for us to count an extra head or two at the dinner table because the children knew they were welcomed. We even had the responsibility of taking neighbors' children to and from school.

Now, we have at least four generations of children on our block, and they have renamed our street "Patton Street Village". Our street is just one block long, but the surrounding blocks love to participate in all the activities that we have.

I am so proud of Patton Street Village.

A Fair Day

by Hazel Nurse

Recently, since the advent of the computer, the many-faceted cell phone, and other wonders of technology, some bookstores have closed.

This, however, makes me remember an extremely happy day many years ago. It was a trip to the annual Philadelphia Book Fair held at the old convention hall.

It was just luck that it was one of the few times in my life that my name was drawn to win a prize.

In that day when books were "king," I won a new set of Americana Encyclopedias, which ferried my family through the ups and downs of life, and still does today!

To put it mildly, this day is forever fair in my memory.

COMING HOME FOR EASTER

by Helen H. Lahr

When my husband sent for me to join him near his Camp Stewart Army Base in Savannah, Georgia, I had never been to the South before. I felt somewhat nervous, although I was ecstatic about joining my new mate. So that I wouldn't

> *"I was ecstatic about joining my new mate."*

be lonely during the day, my husband's army buddy arranged to have his bride join him. Louise, her name, was from North Carolina. She was a very sweet girl, and we were compatible right away.

I had heard about the discrimination in the South, but I felt more at ease with Louise. When we went into town, we went to the back of the bus. Inwardly, I seethed, but I was not the type to make a scene. When we entered the shops (my husband had told me to purchase an Easter outfit) the salespersons were very polite. There were separated dressing rooms. The one we entered had "Colored" over the doorway. The salespersons chatted with us, asking where I was from. I answered in a polite way because they were nice. Louise was very comfortable because she was used to the laws of the South.

When my husband came home that evening I showed him my new outfit and hat. He said they were pretty. I can remember exactly what they looked like. The suit was lilac and so was the hat (a pillbox with veiling over it). The blouse was white with a lace collar and cuffs. My gloves were white lace.

My husband made reservations on the Silver Meteor train. This was a luxury train with dark red velvet drapes and matching carpeting. Needless to say, I felt elegant strolling on my husband's arm, past the people who did not have reservations, and boarding the train.

When we arrived in Philadelphia, we rode to my parent's home in a cab. You can imagine how happy my parents and my sister were to see us. And my in-laws had come down from Lancaster! There was a sumptuous Easter dinner and happiness all around.

"happiness all around" During the next week we motored to Lancaster and spent a couple of days before going back to Savannah. What memories!

WHY ASK WHY?

by Henrietta Faust

Why is it when any black person does any crime anywhere in the world, all blacks are made to feel collective guilt?! But when a white person does a catastrophic, terroristic, cascading-to-major-chaos act of mass murder, whites make excuses, show no angry hate, and never show racist angst!? And no hate is shown for the entire other white race by the dominant race. Look at Columbine, this movie guy, on 7/20/2012 at 12:00 a.m., in a Colorado, Denver/Aurora suburb. And what about the guy overseas? Mass murders! At no time were all whites called "Animals!" Neither was any hate for an entire race shown. No anger, no hate, and absolutely no angst are ever used against the dominant race when the minorities get this treatment all the time! Why is this? Why?

LIFE LIKE A DREAM

by Michael Chan Man-Tin

I was born in a beautiful country, Soo Chow, China, which is the most beautiful "garden" country in Asia. Many visitors from the world visit to see the gardens. There are different flower shows for the four seasons throughout the year.

I left my country when I was seventeen years old and my first stop was Shanghai. By 1949, I left Shanghai after staying there for five years. Then, I went to Hong Kong by train—it took five days by train. They speak a different dialect in Hong Kong—Cantonese—so I took night classes to learn both Cantonese and English. After seven years I started my own company in the garment industry and worked very hard. My daughter came here to go to school at the University of Pennsylvania. I stayed in Hong Kong for fifty years before moving here to be with my daughter.

My wonderful life, it is just like a dream! I never thought I could leave my country in Asia for another life in America.

"My wonderful life, it is just like a dream!"

A Church War

by Mo McCooper

One of the public school kids at the playground invited us to play basketball against his friends from Ardmore, PA, in a building called "YMCA." We had a great time and were invited to play in a league. The baskets at our Catholic school were only six feet high, and we refused to play there.

Monday at school, a priest came in and told us that the YMCA was a Protestant organization and that it would be a mortal sin to join and dangerous to our souls to even play in the league. We had to take a letter home to be signed by a parent that we would not be allowed back to the YMCA.

Later that week, we were taken by one of the parents to another building in Ardmore called the Knights of Columbus, where we were taught shuffleboard and watched the men play cards, shoot darts, and drink beer. They had no leagues for us to join.

None of us ever talked about religion at the playground, but we were beginning to see how important it was to adults. Fortunately, my dad had a great sense of humor about everything, even religion, so life went on. Seventh grade continued.

"my dad had a great sense of humor"

PHEASANT AND RABBIT

by Mo McCooper

In Ireland my grandfather was born in Tyrone County, where all boys learned to fish and hunt while following the dogs to surprise the prey. Among my fond memories is my dad explaining to me the special talent of pointers, setters, retrievers, and springers, who lived in kennels behind our family bar.

With a child's bow and arrow I'd walk way behind the men who would be reaching to fire their rifles at growling pheasants, wild rabbits, and squirrels startled off by the hiding "BIRD DOGS." This was very serious business. Usually three or four cars or pickup trucks took dogs and men a few hours west from Philadelphia to Chester County, where the Pennsylvania Dutch farmers

> *"This was very serious business"*

would allow us to hunt on their land. Sometimes they would invite us in for lunch, which was always more food than I ever saw at a dinner table anywhere else, plus pumpkin or rhubarb pie and ice cream for dessert.

I love those people. In writing this I realize that no other kids were ever with us. I never realized how incredibly lucky I was. Later, a sixteen-year-old boy came along, but that's a story for another day.

CULTURAL SHOCK

by Norman Cain

In the fall of 1965, I completed military police training at Fort Gordon in Augusta, Georgia, and was assigned to the 549th police unit in the Republic of Panama.

En route to my destination, I stopped at the Charleston, South Carolina, Air Force base. There in the canteen, I saw a buxom, tall, and dark black woman who evidently worked there and who spoke with a West Indian accent. I assumed that she was of Gullah ethnicity: black folk who had been isolated on islands in the vicinity of North Carolina, South Carolina, and Georgia for well over 100 years. They retained many elements of African culture and language patterns.

When I arrived at Fort Kobbe Air Force Base on the Pacific Ocean side of Panama, I received a shock! For in the canteen, I saw a tall, buxom, black, woman who evidently worked there and who seemingly spoke the same dialect as her look-a-like in Charleston. Just when I thought the cultural shock was through with me, another incident happened! Waiting at an outside train station for a train to take me to the Atlantic side of Panama, I encountered twelve young shoeshine boys.

Eleven had the physical attributes that we associated with Hispanics and one had attributes associated with blacks. When the black kid spoke rapid Spanish, I could not believe my ears. I had been accustomed to the way things were in America and what I had seen and heard in the media.

The trip to Panama opened my eyes up to the fact that language and culture can transcend ethnic groups and geographical locations.

"language and culture

can transcend"

THE BIG BOYS AND GIRLS

by Norman Cain

I was initially raised on the north side of West Philadelphia in a section known as Mill Creek... which we called "the bottom." I lived on Olive Street, which was near 43rd and Lancaster Avenue. It was an alley-like street with small row houses. The neighbors (no matter their ages) truly cared and practiced a "chain of command" based upon age.

Boys and girls in their teens would actually be—for a lack of a better term—the "bosses" of those who were at least two years younger. Sometimes these teens would work in a group and take us to the Christmas and Mummers parades, Teague Island, The Philadelphia Thrill Show at Franklin Field, Kelly's Pool, Gustine Lake, and other places.

When you did something out of character, they verbally chastised you, but you could look up to these teens and always depend upon them. A big guy named Shorty actually saved me from drowning in six feet of water at Kelly's Pool. Barbara Eason, who earned a Ph.D. in Education and became principal of McMichael Elementary School, mentored me throughout my formative years. When I became fifteen, I moved to 56th and Lancaster Avenue, and the older kids became young adults and married. Occasionally, I would run into one of these former big guys and girls and remind them of how it used to be, and how much I appreciate them.

SUMMER TRIP

by Norman Cain

My younger sister and I always knew that our roots were closely akin to South Carolina, as we were constantly reminded of the state—which was referred to as "Home" by my extended family from the region, who were basically migrants that relocated to Philadelphia during the Second World War era.

Often times, they would fondly engage in conversation of how much fun it was in the good old days and like the greats of old, give historical facts in the oral tradition about those who had been deceased for decades. And then there were the family gatherings during the holiday periods, where tales about the homeland were rich and bountiful. Also there

"historical facts in the oral tradition"

was the occasional phone call from a relative to render the latest news. Around Christmastime my mother's mother would send a fruit cake, cones, walnuts, pecans, and crackling bread that always arrived in a box that was covered by thick brown paper that was secured tightly by tape and durable string. Relatives were always staying at our house until they could get a job and secure lodgings.

At the end of each school year my parents would send my younger sister and me to our grandparents in South Carolina. This arrangement lasted from the last week of June until the day after Labor Day. We would work on their tobacco and cotton farm. Additionally, we got a chance to embrace a different lifestyle. I

"We got a chance to embrace a different lifestyle"

enjoyed and looked forward to this facet of my life, as my temperament was more in sync with nature than the swift pace of the city. The preparation leading up to our departure, the train ride, and arriving at our destination have produced profound "coming of age" memories that I will forever cherish.

First came the period of physical preparation that encompassed the gathering of suitable clothing, food for the trip, and an interview with the travel aide representative who would arrange for me and my sister to reach our destination by ourselves. Several days before we left, my mother would take us to Lancaster Avenue to shop for the items that we would need for our trip such as underwear, sneakers, short pants, shirts, jeans, ties, shirts both collared and T, toothpaste, hair grease, combs, and for recreation on the train we would stop by the Five and Dime store for coloring books and crayons as well as comics. Finally, we were taken to Philadelphia's 30th Street Station.

Once there, we would be taken into a neat and spacious office where the same very nice white woman who we encountered for years and years, and who always wore a nice dress to accent her thin frame, would engage in a general conversation to ascertain whether or not we would be able to make the journey by ourselves. After this encounter, we always received a nametag that we promised to wear until we reached our destination. The trip would always be scheduled for the following night.

The trip itself was generally around eleven o'clock, so about seven o'clock we would be ushered to bed for two hours of restless turning before we dressed. At the prescribed time a yellow cab would arrive, and we would board it and begin our fifteen-minute ride to the train station.

"Their presence was tightly woven into the culture of America"

Railroads were a different entity in those days. In fact, their presence was tightly woven into the culture of America. An example would be the numerous motion pictures that had their plots revolve around the railroad. Also, it was common for boys to receive model train sets for Christmas.

In my case, it was particularly paramount because my father worked for the railroad, and it was because he was able to get free tickets for his family to areas like New York and Washington D.C. that my sister and I were in a better position to travel to and from South Carolina each year. Periodically, a burst of steam would give a hissing sound and rapidly emanate from the bottom of the locomotive, turning into a thick misty cloud. The train would jerk suddenly and then slowly begin to move. The clash of steel wheels against rail produced thick sparks that would disappear into the heated atmosphere. The whistle would sound, long, high-pitched, yet hollow. Before long, the train would be speeding down the tracks at a high speed.

THE GREAT NEIGHBORHOOD DEBATE OF 1955

by Norman Cain

In 1955 when I was thirteen years old, I began to notice a different religious group in the neighborhood. They called themselves the Nation of Islam. The men dressed in black suits, white shirts, and bowties, and the women wore white scarves and long white dresses. They denounced Christianity, refrained from eating pork, disdained drugs and alcohol, sold a newspaper called Mohammed Speaks, had a holy book called the Koran, and called the white man a "blue-eyed devil." Only a few people listened to the proponents of the new religion. However, there were two respected people in the neighborhood, a devout Christian woman and a man who had recently joined the Nation of Islam, who would debate the authenticity of the new faith.

On several consecutive Sunday afternoons in the spring, these debaters would face each other on a long, narrow street, which was no more than an alley bordered on each side by scant pavements that led up to micro-mini townhouses. Both pavements would be filled with people who were looking forward to a diversion from the occasional fist fight, stumbling drunks, men dressed like cowboys mounted upon regal horses, or the roaring motorcycles that sometimes graced our street. The debaters would be about 10 feet apart and stood erect with their eyes locked. The battle that was about to ensue remained as one of the high noon "shootouts" that were prevalent in cowboy films during the era.

While I cannot recall the exact dialogue that ensued during this occasion, I can hypothetically say that it started with Mr. Wilson saying, "Good afternoon, Mrs. Cain" with the confidence of a man who owned a barber shop, convenience store, and barbecue restaurant. "I see you've got your white communion dress on today." He continued, "The women in the Nation of Islam wear white too, but for a different reason." He waited briefly for a response that was not forthcoming, and continued speaking, "You're wearing white for the wrong reason."

Before he could go any further, Mrs. Cain retorted,

"I'm not the nation of whatever you call it."

"I'm not in the 'Nation' of whatever you call it. I am a soldier in the army of the Lord. You've got a nerve to talk about my dress. I serve the body and blood of Christ with this dress on." The crowd was silent, amazed at this little woman who did not back down from the man who was clearly a foot-and-a-half taller than her.

"Blood of Christ? You're wrong. Everything about Christianity is wrong. The honorable Elijah Mohammed will tell you that."

"Who? What about Jesus Christ? Were your kinfolk wrong? They were God-fearing Christians. Were your mother and father wrong? Were your grandparents wrong? No, they were not wrong."

Mr. Wilson did not respond. He vacated his position and went into his house. Also, Mrs. Cain went into her dwelling, and the spectators tried to rationalize this turn of events. The short-statured, dark woman became the champion of the women watching and listening to the action unfolding in front of them, for she had the nerve to stand up to this man during a time when women were supposed to stay in their place.

Why did Mrs. Cain resort to including Mr. Wilson's family into the debate? Why did Mr. Wilson leave defeated? The answer to these questions lay in the fact that the debaters were both from a rural South Carolina township called Pamplico, and although he was clearly eight years her senior, they were friends. Their families had known each other for decades. In fact, it was Mr. Wilson who had smuggled Mrs. Cain from South Carolina in 1939, when she ran away from college to marry her fiancé who was already in Philadelphia. He smuggled her to the destination to reunite with her love. Mr. Wilson's losing of the debate was caused by his being reminded of the customs of his ancestors.

"reunite with her love"

Eventually, he left the Nation of Islam. It was not what he thought it would be. As for Mrs. Cain, she remained a Christian for the rest of her life. However, three out of her five grandsons became affiliated with Islam.

Incidentally, Mrs. Cain was my mother. That is why I know the intricacies of the preceding story so well.

YESTERDAY'S PEOPLE

by Bernice Moore

I am always drawing pictures, even back when I was in school. A lot of the time I drew difficult things like houses, trees, cars, boats, and many other things.

It's fun when you know how to draw different things. You can see so many things if you keep your mind on what is really happening. You cannot live in this world alone, with so many things to do and see.

> *"You cannot live in this world alone"*

Everything has changed since the war years; we still have wars in different places. Some people still can't get along, but I'm glad more people are like flowers: different colors, different breeds, and different worlds.

TO RACE OR ERASE

by Hazel Nurse

Perhaps phone calls, fliers, and several television reminders all occur to emphasize the importance of filing the census report—which I had already done—on time. Can you help me with the proper answer to race? Years ago in a genealogy class I traced my family tree back to 1928, using records, archives, and oral information. If race could be mathematically correct, I am only black and possibly from Ghana and other parts of Africa. I am only American Indian from a great-grandmother who was called a full-blooded Powhatan Indian of Virginia. I am only Asian from an artist son's rendition of my Aunt's eyes' folds. I am Irish from my maternal great-grandfather, Charles Bell, who kept in touch with my grandmother, who was also his daughter.

Since this was just the beginning of my research, should we embrace the term race, or erase it in the census?

"should we embrace the term race, or erase it"

STEP BY STEP

by Michael Chan Man-Tin

My life passes quickly. I have been in this city five years now. I am wondering how I myself can be settled down here. I have to thank God for leading the way to follow. And I am still being led. I have a lot of things to learn and found the people here are very friendly and help me, step by step, to enjoy the life from the society and hopefully to know more and more of this society.

I am happy to learn more and more from the friends here, and thank you for the help.

Best wishes!

"I am happy to learn more and more from the friends here"

SEE IF YOU CAN FEEL THIS

by Henrietta Faust

See if you can feel this:
Real as a cold wind...
A cold wind that is out to blow.
As real as poverty,
But how real now is rich?
Is the wind in your face on a yacht in Monte Carlo
really different from
The icy, painful, stinging wind of a pissy New York alley
In a cardboard box of the homeless?
Is anything as real as poverty?
In a nation of excess, opulence and decadence,
The cold-blooded obsession of riches and power are
toys.
And now the successful raises up a standard of
double-dipping
But Nothing
But poverty is real.
Nothing is as real.
Look at how
The U.S.A. gave financial bail-outs.
Now how many still woke up in poverty?
They went to bed 10/14/2008 kings of the hill
And woke up 10/15/2008 broke and lost
Without new jobs and money to deal with $2,000-a-day
spas!
One foot in poverty and the other in Hell.
And as real as poverty, but how real now is rich?
And a cold wind is a cold wind all over the world.

4

Family

The Things I Want My Grandkids to Know

by Beatrice Newkirk

The things I want my grandkids to know: how I raised them and how I was raised; things I did in my time of growing up. Some people were going through hard times. Things were not easy. In my early years, we had no television. We did the best we could in my days.

"Things were not easy"

Raising twelve kids was not too easy, either. Trying to decide what to feed them and how to dress them. Me and their father trying to make ends meet. In my coming up, we had no choice of what we wanted to eat or what we wanted to wear.

I have no complaints about them. They have made me very proud. All have finished school. Everyone doing the right thing. I thank God for my kids and grandkids and for my great-grands. 57 grands – 27 greats!

A Woman Who Cared About Children

by Beatrice Moore

My foster mother was a person who cared for children. They would send the child who was the worst off. Some were ill and disabled, but she would take the time to love them all. They would send children that nobody wanted. There were

> *"she would take the time to love them all"*

some who could not walk or talk, and she would take the time to help them. I would help her all the time. There was a boy who they said would never walk, but in time she had him walking. There were a lot of unwanted children. She was a good foster mother. All the children that were sent to her in bad shape, when they left they would be walking and talking.

My foster mother died in 1950. At the time, I was married and my husband was in the army. I miss her so much. She taught me a lot of things to do in my lifetime. I will never forget her.

From Frisco to Art

by Brenda Bailey

My Aunt Paula was a singer in the "big band era," and she sang and played piano with many bands like Duke Ellington, Count Basie, and more. She had a Chihuahua named Frisco that she carried everywhere she went. When she was on stage she left him in her dressing room because he did what all Chihuahuas do—bark, bark, bark. When she returned, he would leave her with a pile of "welcome back."

One night after a social gathering at our house, when everybody was asleep, Frisco decided to go through the trash, and he found some spicy Mexican food—which he ate. That morning, he woke up everybody with his screams of pain. Paula immediately took him to the vet and after several hours of trying to relieve his pain, the vet informed Paula that the humane thing was to put him to sleep. My aunt kissed Frisco and went to her car where she screamed, hollered, raged, and cried for over an hour. She was inconsolable. She never got over Frisco.

Shortly after this incident, she was scheduled to perform in Europe, and she never returned to the U.S. When we asked why, she said that black entertainers were respected and appreciated more by the audiences overseas. The same statement made by Josephine Baker and Tina Turner and others.

I don't know when Paula transferred her love for Frisco to art, but my mother started receiving cards and letters with pictures she had drawn—some in color, some pen, and some charcoal. We were impressed, but she was always so talented. When she died, she had been living abroad for over thirty years in Sweden. Her personality was such that people gravitated to her, so she had many, many friends to whom she left her personal belongings. I myself have copies of original drawings.

I have been thinking about my own life—if I had the time, what things would I transfer from and to, and how would I make a difference?

"how would I make a difference?"

I think I would like to be a history teacher—exploring with my students the who, what, where, when, why, and how of our world around us. And, I want to be called Mo Bee Bee

The Coal Stove

by Bri Kurmue

We lived in a very drafty house and in the winter, my mom would say, "Becke (Bri), go downstairs (to the basement) and put (3) shovels of coal on the fire, open the top door, and close the damper." Of course I would forget and do the exact opposite. Eventually, the radiators would begin to feel barely warm, whereas before, they were steaming hot, and the house would begin to cool off to a chill.

My poor, tired mommy would have to go to the basement and coax the furnace to fire up again (inside would be burning ashes), using newspaper and sometimes charcoal, if we had any, before it would build up once more.

She was soooooo tired from mothering (6) children, preparing (3) meals a day for us, making sure our clothes were ready for school the next day, and that we had done our homework. She would fall into bed... exhausted!! And although she slept, she did not rest, because she was still on duty. If any of her babies needed her during the night, she was always available.

She was a good mother

She loved us.

I miss her very much.

THREE MILE WALK AND TALK, TALK, TALK

by Bri Kurmue

Good Fun Mother's Day!

Mother's Day was a very lovely day. It was beautiful weather and a nice sunshiny day. Some would call it sweater weather in a.m. and almost balmy by afternoon. My daughter and I "walked for the cure." There were soooo many people on the Parkway: men, women, boys, girls, pets, and bikes. The mood was upbeat and absolutely infectious… there was laughter and excitement in the air. It was tangible, it was moving, and it was surrounding; you could almost touch it in the atmosphere. Practically everyone spoke to each other and shouted out "Happy Mother's Day" to all the females. It was loads of fun.

My daughter Meiyata and I walked and talked. Her personality is tongue-in-cheek funny. She can bring laughter from me. She is very beautiful with a dark complexion and a healthy body like most Liberian women. Beautiful teeth with super-shaped lips, a smooth, perfectly clear face, and very expressive eyes that actually seem to speak to you out loud.

"She is very beautiful"

She has a strong sense of self, progressing toward her personal goals and achieving her desires in a sensible manner. Her personal relationship with the Creator started in early childhood. She holds meaningful conversations and is a good listener. Overall, she is a nice person to know and has a dynamite affection for her family. As her mother I would like to say, my daughter is special to me and I love my firstborn girl a whole lot. She is a gentle soul and someone the earth needs!

PEACE!

MOMMY'S SECRET

by Hattie Lee Ellerbe

I cannot beat around the bush... as I write from week to week, all of you know that my children are my achievements. I could not be more proud of any three people in the whole world. They are my life, my best friends, "the wind beneath my wings."

In case they read this note, the secret is out; you are all "mommy's favorites." The guessing game is over. Now don't fight over me... who wants me this weekend?

"who wants me this weekend?"

A LETTER TO MY PATERNAL GRANDMOTHER

by Hattie Lee Ellerbe

This letter is to my paternal grandmother. My father was her only child.

Dear Grandma,

Did I ever tell you that I love you?

I remember, as a child, you always lived in the same house with us and shared in our wellbeing. You made our clothes, and clothes for our dolls. We loved to visit you on the third floor and go through all your treasures.

Although Mamma and Daddy were Baptist, we loved to go to Mother Bethel AME Church with you. You would love to know that I am still a member there. You instilled the love of God in us and wanted us to be nice, clean, smart, and good little girls, and later young ladies.

When Momma died at age twenty-eight (in child birth), you stepped right in and took over the parenting of the five of us, ages newborn to nine years old. I loved you so much then, but I don't remember saying so.

However, many years later when I was forty-one years old (1974), as I was saying goodnight to you, I kissed you and said I love you and you looked up at me and smiled and breathed your last breath in my arms.

About Grandmom

by Hattie Lee Ellerbe

On Friday afternoon it was time for Mr. Ferguson to come to our house. He was our music teacher. For $2.50 a week per household, he taught all of us.

Grandmom was determined to have all of us learn to play the piano. Growing up, we always had a piano in our house. I never really learned to play, but three of my sisters did.

Grandmom was so proud of us; she had us singing at church and anytime we had company at home. I am the middle child of the five sisters, and I admit, I was different. Grandmom wanted us all to be little ladies. I was a "tomboy" and was always having accidents by falling down or hurting myself. I was always on punishment.

Everyone, including myself, thought Grandmom "picked on me" and whipped me the most.

We had sufficient clothing, and Grandmom worked very hard as a factory worker to see that we never went to bed hungry. She stressed education and religion. I never missed a day of school in twelve years.

It wasn't until I became a grown-up that Grandmom and I became close. In later years, November 26, 1974, around 8:00 p.m., she died in my arms, with a smile on her face as I tearfully whispered: I love you.

THRIFTY TO A T

by Hazel Nurse

At the seashore when the five-cent postage stamp still existed, winters were desolate and times were tough. However, we welcomed Grandmom to join our clan of five children plus Mom and Daddy.

"when the five-cent postage stamp still existed"

Declaring that she was an expert chef, my mother not only concocted economical dishes such as tempting codfish cakes made with an abundance of mashed potatoes, but also sold homemade lemon pies to make ends meet.

Tea in our family was much desired but not given to us children. That poor tea bag took a trip first to Dad's cup, then to Mom, and lastly to Grandmom. But I have news for you: Grandmom extended the life the tea bag by placing it in the refrigerator for the next participant.

One of the Things I'm Most Proud of in My Life

by Helen H. Lahr

I say one of the things of which I am most proud, because there are many things in life that I am proud of. I will write about number one.

My sister and I were very blessed to have a mother and father like our parents. We couldn't have had better parents. Irene and I were surrounded by love. Our dad was a construction worker who always provided for our family. He never let our mother go to work and she took good care of us. In those days there were no electric

"washing clothes on a washboard"

refrigerators or washing machines. During our very early years I can remember my mother washing clothes on a washboard and heating the iron on a stove with wood. She went to the butcher's on South Street every other day.

Every day she made hot biscuits for us. I can also remember how she made starch for our dresses and our dad's shirts, and also the borders of our pillowcases and sheets. In order to press these articles they sprinkle and fold them, and put them in a special laundry basin.

She wanted her family to look nice. Our mother never left us with anyone; she took care of her "girls" herself. When Daddy was home he liked to watch us play with our friends from the neighborhood while he sat back and smoked his pipe. There wasn't a morning before work that he didn't come into our bedroom to "look in on the girls" as he put it.

His pet name for our mother was "Doll Baby." They had grown up in the same small country town; they were married at the ages of fifteen and seventeen and were inseparable.

So you can see what beautiful parents Diane and I were blessed to have. They shaped the manner in which I raised my children.

MY LOVELY PARENTS

by Helen H. Lahr

My parents were born in North Carolina in the same country town. The little girl, who was to become the mother of my sister and me, was the daughter of the area minister of three small churches. My father was the son of a farmer. So they always, always knew each other.

When they were seventeen and fifteen years of age, they married. Later, they came north to Philadelphia. In the ensuing years my sister and I were born. We were a closely knit family.

"We were a close knit family"

My dad always called Irene and me "his girls." He never went to work without coming into our bedroom doorway to check on us.

When Christmas came around, it was really a time of fun and expectations. We really believed that there was a Santa Claus and that he came down the chimney.

Mother began to cook the goodies several weeks ahead of the holidays. I can remember Mother having us help to pick the meat out of the walnut shells, which she had cracked with a nutcracker. Mother was to use the walnuts in a walnut cake. Usually she also baked a coconut cake and a chocolate layer cake.

Sweet potato, lemon meringue, and pumpkin pies were also added to the goodies. Oh, yes, I almost forgot to add butter cookies. Needless to say, our home was full of delicious aromas.

My father would pretend that he was sneaking into the kitchen or dining room to snitch some of the cookies. Of course, my sister Irene and I were on the receiving end of some of them. You might know that my mother was well aware of what was going on—pretending that she didn't.

Christmas Eve, we were sent to bed early. Naturally, we were very nervous. We would lie awake for quite sometime before we could go to sleep.

Christmas morning Irene and I awakened early and raced down the stairs to the living room, where the Christmas tree and our gifts were.

Our parents were smiling. Years later, when we no longer believed in Santa Claus, they told us that sometimes they stayed up all night. They were trying to make things nice for us.

"truly blessed"

My sister and I were truly blessed to have such wonderful parents.

JUMP ROPE

by Loretta Gaither

I had a jump rope. I remember jumping this rope and playing hopscotch. My mother would call me to eat, and I told my dad that I was afraid to go because I was afraid of the dog; I wasn't afraid. I just wanted my dad to pick me up and carry me. It was *"I was Daddy's girl."* our private time and he would ask me about my day. Our private time! I was Daddy's girl. I loved both of my parents but this memory is special.

A SAILOR BOY'S SWEETHEART

by Mo McCooper

During World War II, my dad's little brother John served in combat with the U.S. Army. The family had a party in a large back room of a restaurant somewhere in Philadelphia. Dad's four brothers and four sisters were there. About six other grandchildren were there too. All the aunts and uncles sang songs and most danced. Suddenly into the room came this big, broad-shouldered lady who must have weighed over two hundred pounds singing, "I'm only a sailor boy's sweetheart, but I'm proud of my sailor boy."

It was Uncle John with pillows stuffed in his coat and a wig

"He was hilarious"

borrowed from a mop. To me he was hilarious. Best of all, he came home safe and sound from the War!

GRANDMOM SHOULD SEE ME NOW

by Hattie Lee Ellerbe

I have been a member of my church since I was five years old. Every Sunday morning as we entered the front door, I would dash up the stairs: two flights. I was so excited.

"I have been a member of my church since I was five years old."

Grandmom would admonish me, "Hattie, stop running up those steps." She couldn't keep up with me.

Now, at age seventy-nine, as I enter the front door, the young people greet me, take me by the arm and say, "Be careful, Miss Hattie" as I almost crawl up the stairs.
Grandmom, I finally stopped running up these steps.

5

Friendship

MORE MEMORIES

by Hattie Lee Ellerbe

On a bright sunny day, I took my best friend, Bobby, for a walk. I don't remember how we got there, but I do remember to this day the location... It was 10th St. and Ridge Ave. This would have been clearly three-and-a-half blocks from home. There was a beer bottling plant on 10th and Callowhill (at Ridge Ave.) where you could watch the bottles go around on a conveyor belt. This was fun to watch. It was fun until we realized that we were lost.

Bobby felt secure because I was older and we could find our way home. I was two months older...we both were three years old. My mother found us both standing on that corner, crying and confused.

All through life this was one of my favorite memories, and Bobby, no matter where he was, was my first and favorite friend.

REMINISCING

by Helen H. Lahr

It all begin when my younger son, Trevor, entered kindergarten. He walked over to an aquarium, and there was a hard-shelled turtle! Trevor was fascinated by the turtle. When school closed for summer vacation, he brought it home with him.

> *"Trevor was fascinated by the turtle"*

As years passed, Trevor bought a rabbit, long and short haired guinea pigs, hamsters, chameleons, white rats, and a cat. Eight hard-shelled turtles were collected from nearby countrysides.

The one thing that I had specifically forbidden him to bring home was a snake. One day, I was in the kitchen when my son came home from junior high school. Instead of coming into the kitchen, as he usually did, he stood in the vestibule with one hand in back of him. I called out to him and asked what was the matter. He didn't answer, so I walked to the vestibule. Tears began to run down Trevor's cheeks. I asked to see what was in his hand. It was a boa constrictor snake. I told him to take it back to the pet shop immediately.

My husband walked in at that moment. I knew he was on his son's side because he had also liked pets as a boy, but he didn't say anything because he knew I was deathly afraid of snakes. Trevor pleaded and pleaded. Finally, I relented when he promised to keep the boa in the basement in an aquarium. Trevor kept the boa through high school and college—he majored in Biology—two years of ROTC, marriage, two children, and becoming Personnel Director of Wyeth Laboratories. It was only when his children were in their teens that the snake caught pneumonia and died.

I neglected to say that Trevor also had three large beehives at the back of his yard. He had joined a national bee organization. At first he bottled honey for the family, but some people actually asked to purchase some. It's surprising the influence that a hard-shelled turtle had in shaping the career of a little boy upon entering kindergarten.

ENJOYING CONVERSATION AND JAZZ

by Josie Miller

Today I arrived at the center really hungry, and I was glad to see the delicious looking meal waiting for me. Most people had finished eating, so there were only the few "regulars" who sit in the cafeteria until the staff asks them to leave.

I sat at a table next to some of these "regulars." I leaned over to ask forgiveness for not bringing the Charlie Parker and Miles Davis CDs that I had promised Sam. He doesn't always hear what I'm saying, so when I finished apologizing to him, he asked, "Where are the CDs you promised?" At one point, Sam left the "regulars" and came to sit with me. Sam's a former jazz musician—a drummer.

We started becoming friends about a month ago when I first started coming to the center. We struck it off when I said I loved to listen to Max Roach and often went to hear Max whenever he was in town; that was over forty years ago. Sam and I laughed and talked and enjoyed each other's company. Then Sam said he wanted us to spend time together on weekends. I suggested he joined my writing group today and I told him all about our writing group. I also told Sam I would write about our lunch conversation in the group. I told him I would not use his real name. We laughed. I enjoyed my lunch.

> *"I loved to listen to Max Roach"*

Arthur Murray was a Friend of Mine

by Loretta Gaither

I knew him from the Uptown Theater and knew he liked to sing and dance. My husband and he were good friends; they went to Simon Gratz High School together. Arthur was a barber. He used to cut hair at a shop at 29th and Dauphin in North Philly. And when I came to Philadelphia Senior Center, that was when I saw him again. Oh, I can't remember how long it was when I saw him last before that.

When I saw him at the senior center after all those years, he *"I love you Loretta!"* kissed me on the cheek right away. He said, "I love you, Loretta," and I said, "I love you back." He loved singing, and he really, really loved our writing class. He is going to be missed by our writing class and the whole center. I am going to miss his smile. I don't know how to put this all into words, but I feel better that I wrote this story about him.

ARTHUR MURRAY

by Mo McCooper

About two years ago, on a day when there was confusion about which room the writing class would be in, we were waiting in the large room next to the registration desk. At the piano on the far side of the room, a man was playing while another man and a lovely lady were singing any words they knew to the songs. After a little while, our writing teacher Benita and I joined in. We were encouraged to sing by a tall, thin man with a winning smile who also played the piano. Arthur Murray made sure we enjoyed ourselves and learned how to harmonize at the same time. Soon after, Arthur joined our writing group, adding his positive attitude and ideas for extra socializing to the agenda. On the charter buses to and from the NPR studios and the Free Library of Philadelphia

"Arthur led us in sing-alongs!"

among others, Arthur led us in sing-alongs! I'll miss him BIG TIME!!!

6

Fun

GROWING UP ON OPAL STREET

by Joan Bunting

From the age of eight years old to the age of seventeen, I lived on a small street called Opal Street. It's spelled Opal, as in the gem, but it was always pronounced O-pal Street.

In the summer during vacation, lots of children from surrounding neighborhoods would come to Opal Street to play. During the morning through early afternoon we played wall ball, three flies, step baseball, play fish, knucks, jacks, marbles, deadman block, cowboys and Indians, and Double Dutch, and we made our own scooters or the original skateboards. We'd get a wooden crate, some old roller skates, a hammer, and nails and get to work.

Every afternoon everyone would disappear and show up again around five or six o'clock, after we'd taken a bath and had eaten our dinner. Then the circle games would begin. We played Down By the Green Apple Tree and Who Stole the Cookie from the Cookie Jar.

Sometimes the waterplug would be turned on as late as twelve and one o'clock at night. The adults would be sitting on the steps watching the young people play. We call or consider those the good old days, but today there are good days as well.

I thank God for those wonderful times and wonderful memories. Also, thank God that He has kept us with these never forgotten memories.

ON A CLOUD

by Loretta Gaither

Last week, we had a play to honor Black History Month. The teacher told me I was a good actor and a good dancer. I was dancing at the front of the stage, and the class was behind me. The audience clapped and screamed, "Go Loretta!" I have arthritis, but I can still dance. It hurts when I sit still, but

"When I dance, I feel better. I feel like I am on a cloud."

when I dance I feel better. I feel like I am on a cloud. I wore low black heels, black pants, and a plain color top, but because I was dancing I felt glamorous and young. Later that night my whole body was achy but I didn't care! I could've gotten up and danced again. I can dance every day, all day. Anytime I hear music at home, or at a store, or even on the sidewalk, my feet start moving. I don't even have to think about it.

THE LOUSY BASEBALL START

by Norman Cain

When I was around fourteen years old, I joined a baseball team, the name of which I've long since forgotten.

The majority of the guys on the team were a few years older than I, and almost to the man played either varsity or junior varsity baseball at their respective high schools. That meant that the team was phenomenal... as baseball was the king of sports in 1957.

While the guys on the team were good, I was not. Actually, I was terrible. I couldn't throw, field, or hit. Most times during our games (at Belmont Plateau, off of 52nd Parkside in West Philadelphia), I kept the scorebook and handled the equipment.

I was terrible, but the guys did not tease or distance themselves from me. They wanted me to be good. Two incidents proved that to me. Once when I was playing center field, a ball was hit in my direction.

"I was terrible, but the guys did not tease or distance themselves from me"

When I looked into the sky at the ball, I was blinded by a blaring sun. I placed my glove over my eyes; and guess what? The ball miraculously fell into my glove. The guys were jumping, screaming, and hollering like we had won the World Series; they were happy for me. I did not tell them that I was shielding myself from the sun. The next incident—concerning me—that led to the team's hysteria had to do with my hitting a home run, after having struck out each time that I was at bat during the season.

I may have been a lousy baseball player, but I received the cheers reserved for superstars.

A Fun Day at Carroll Park

by Aileen Jefferson

"Look, Mother, there's an empty bench!"
Such a lovely sunny day and almost every bench was taken.

Every mom in Philly must be there with their young ones, and as I looked about it seemed they were.

Sunshine here... sunshine there... sunshine everywhere.
A beautiful spot for my young bunny rabbits, with shady trees.

> *"Sunshine here...sunshine there... sunshine everywhere."*

My luck today!

I believe the baby is smiling. And guess what, mommy is smiling too... green grass, purple violets, yellow daffodils, and me and my little bunny.

As I pushed the carriage I saw my best friend smiling across the verdant expanse at me, and that makes two of us reveling in nature's bounty.

DANCING AT THE BEAUTY SCHOOL

by Loretta Gaither

I was getting my hair done at the salon, and my hair was just finished. And I was getting up to go when I heard music outside in the lobby. So I started dancing. I was the only one dancing—people came from their stations to watch

> *"I heard music outside in the lobby."*

me. And the hairdresser teachers were all clapping and laughing and said I was good. They gave me a button: it was gold with a star and the background had the salon's name on it—Empire.

7

Identity and Self Expression

Growing Up is Hard to Do
The Best Day of My Life So Far
This Morning
Today
The Woman I Am
Being Small

Growing Up is Hard to Do

by Hattie Lee Ellerbe

In spite of the many hardships my family endured coming up, I never wanted to be "grown." I wanted to stay a child and play, play, play. I thought if I could do as I pleased, I could be happy for the rest of my life.

I quickly learned, as a teenager, that this was not possible. The responsibilities of getting an education and completing high school became a priority for me. Being a middle child always made me special. I was little sister to my two older sisters and big sister to my two little sisters.

Since I was the tallest of all my sisters, hand-me-down dresses were always too short, and in my wildest imagination too worn... but I had to wear them anyway. My two older sisters were always nice and neat. My two younger sisters were always nice and neat. Because I was a tomboy wearing four-year-old hand-me-downs, there was nothing to hand down to my little sisters. Grandmom never let me forget how rough I was on shoes and clothes. If I hadn't been so proud of my even, white teeth, I would have told her that the clothes were worn out when I got them.

Being a middle child was different for me because I was the only one out of five sisters who graduated in the fall. The other four graduated in June. Grandmom was horrified and declared she never heard of anybody graduating in the winter...even though I managed to do it 3 times!

"No one ever thought I would grow up to be a girl."

I rode bikes, played marbles, boxed boys, and played boy games. No one ever thought I would grow up to be a girl. One of my male friends even said to me, "Hattie Mae, if I had known you were going to grow up to be a girl, I would have introduced you to some boys!"

The Best Day of My Life So Far

by Norman Cain

Today I feel great because of you
And honey is the color of my ecstasy

It tastes like a whiff of fresh, fresh air
Garnished with the scent of roses/daffodils

It sounds like the sweet strains of violins riding
Gentle winds

It feels like soothing vibrations massaging my stressed
Out lonely soul, making it whole

It looks like a memory and heartfelt emotions that
The portrait of a master artist evokes

"It smells sweet"

It smells sweet like the smile of your grandmother
When she had not seen you for a while.

THIS MORNING

by Patricia Williams

Yesterday I grasped earth's bosom, bare
Cold, shivering, withstanding
The elements of that season
This morning my branches give
New green birth
A wren perched on my limb
Sings joyfully
Tulips caress my base
A new dawn, another season

TODAY

by Patricia Williams

I opened the front door,
Inhaled the freshness of the morning,
Bathed in its dew,
Absorbed the sun's bright rays,
Plucked the rainbow from the sky,
Garbed myself in its colors,
Sang along with a robin,
Looked across the street,
Called to my neighbor.
Good morning Mr. Jones,
It's so good to be alive.

THE WOMAN I AM

by Louella Coplon

The woman I am hides deep in me, beneath the woman I seem to be.

She hides away from strangers and those known to her passing by.

She goes her way. And they go their way.

For those who love me dearly, look beneath the woman I seem to be and see only me!

"The woman I am hides deep in me"

BEING SMALL

by Joan Bunting

When I was a child, and even in my teen and adult years, I was very skinny. I believe I took after my father. Even as a full grown adult, I grew up to be taller than him. I was told he never weighed more than 99 pounds. I don't know whether that was true or not, but he was a small man in stature and size.

Two of my foster mothers tried to make me fatten up! One gave me lard and sugar sandwiches. They didn't taste bad, except when it was goose grease or lard.

The second one gave me lard and sugar or butter and sugar sandwiches. When we had chicken for dinner, I always got the next to the meatiest part of the chicken, which is the drumstick. My younger brother, who is younger than me, got the breast. She had raised him since he was 10 months old, so he got the best. She even bought a case of beer for me. But if I remember correctly, I only got one or two beers out of the whole case. Later I learned that beer is supposed to be fattening. Beer, like ice cream, bloats you and is false healthy weight.

When I was in junior high school, the school nurse told me that if I didn't eat, I was going to die. If she only knew how much I did eat. Of course I was called names such as Skinny Minnie, Boney Joany, and others by other children.

"I was called names"

In my teens, after I had my dinner, I'd stand in the front door and try to push my stomach out to make it look like I had one, but of course it didn't work.

Now I have developed a stomach. Do I want it? No. I can't get rid of it to save my life. But, I'm okay. It could be bigger, much bigger, than it is.

8

Life Lessons and Philosophy

LIFE IS SO WONDERFUL

by Arthur Murray

When you stop and think a little bit, life is so sweet. Lots of times we don't really value it as much as we could. When you stop and look at another person's situation, some are happy, sad, troubled, mad, or unhappy with their life. But look at the bright side: we're still here. All we have to do is love one another much more. The world is here for you and me. My experience in life is loving each and every person, because the energy you get back is so great. Love— and this world is full of love—is what the world needs, love and understanding. Just let go, with all the love you can give, and cherish the love in return.

"love one another"

Keep up the good work.

ADVICE ON H AND H

by Brenda Bailey

To expose ourselves to heartache and heartbreak is an emotion we can all identify with—but how we react depends on our life experiences. When you are young and your heart is broken, you ask yourself, "What did I do?" "Why me?" And you cry, can't sleep, can't eat. Life seems so dark. I felt the same, when it happened to me at a young age. I cried, it seemed, for days. Couldn't sleep. Couldn't eat. I thought I would never be the same, and I wasn't. I

"I was stronger"

was stronger. And the day I smelled the bacon cooking, I was so hungry.

I ate. I was tired and needed to sleep. And the next day, when I awakened, I knew I had made it and I'd be OK.

As we become developed in age, older, we have more heartaches and heartbreaks. Like when we lose a loved one or a beloved pet or a favorite earring that has sentimental value. But I know it is only temporary. I had the power to survive. Our Creator has given us a resilient spirit, to stand and not fall, to bend and not break. So, like the song says, "Pick yourself up, dust yourself off, and start all over again."

And, when all else fails, have a piece of bacon.

A Rose is a Rose

by Helen H. Lahr

Some years ago, members of my family and I were riding through a certain neighborhood when, after seeing a lot of very lovely homes, we came upon a decrepit old house. Grass and weeds and trees surrounded it. Some of the windows were broken and the basement windows (also partly broken) were covered with debris.

Then, to my amazement, I saw a beautiful rose growing up out of all that chaos. To me, it was one of the most lovely sights I had ever seen!

Afterwards, a line from a poem came to mind.

> *"Blossom where you are planted"*

"Blossom where you are planted."
What this tells is that no matter where we live or what the situation, we can attain the goals that we have set for ourselves. All we have to do is try.

VISION

by Joe Garrison

One afternoon I was getting on a bus, waiting for a seat when some well-meaning person offered to take me to a seat. However, he sat me on someone's lap. I was embarrassed and the person I sat on was angry. I in turn was angry at the person who supposedly was trying to help me. I could smell alcohol on his breath. He said to me, "What are you arguing with me about? You can't even see!"

Another incident was when someone asked me if I wished I could see. The moral of the story is I do not have physical sight, but I believe I can see. Movies and television are just as enjoyable *"I believe I can see."* to me as they are to you. If I am in your presence or I experience being with you, then I see you. If I understand what you are telling me, then I see. To see means to understand.

THE CHANGING SEASONS

by Mary Angelucci

Say Goodbye to yesterday
tomorrow is at the door
those lazy, lazy Summer days
are gone and Fall is here
once more.

I reminisce about days
gone by but look forward to
the new,
For each new season brings a new beginning,
And challenges to me
and you.

So no matter what the season
whether its Winter, Spring, Summer or Fall,
Each one comes with an opportunity to make it the
best one of all.

SUCCESS

by Norman Cain

Life at times can have us down flat, can become unbearably grim, making us leery and ill at ease within. Life can be full of sudden setbacks and rigid obstacles, but attaining one's goals is truly possible.

Success in life takes perseverance and a will to achieve, and in yourself you must truly believe. We must tightly clutch and wield the stick of stick-to-it-ness and make every day our best against the pain of hardship. For hardship is only a test of this life that measures whether one will transcend its perils and strife.

Hardship is a test that all humanity must successfully *"mind over matter"* pass to reach the goals and dreams needed to be amassed. So profusely project mind over matter, and your wants and needs will be served on life's golden platter.

A SPECTACULAR SIGHT

by Helen H. Lahr

On this past Tuesday I got up, as usual, to come into the Senior Center, and as we (my daughter and I) came out of the house, it started pouring. As we proceeded down I-95, it didn't get any better. Sue could barely see well enough to drive the car, and to top that off it was very dark. Finally, we reached Philadelphia and you wouldn't believe it, but the rain suddenly stopped and the sun came out. Then, when we turned onto Lombard Street, my eyes suddenly saw a beautiful sight—the trees, which had been asleep and brown the week before, were all in bloom. Some were pink, some were white, and others were deep red. What a sight! What a nice way to have my early morning turn out.

"the trees... were all in bloom"

THE BEST THING I HAVE LEARNED IN MY LIFE

by Gogo Jenny Williams

It took many years and it seemed that I kept butting my head against hardened walls. I learned that you can begin again; you can forgive, turn around, pick up the pieces, and learn from your mistakes.

Bad decisions – I've made a few. Missed opportunities – yes, I've missed a few. Trusted the untrustworthy – yes I did. Experiencing encounters of the 3rd and 4th kind made me a better human being – the so-called failures became stepping stones to my success, the backbone that enabled me to stand up and face life, not hide in a corner when it seemed that my world crumbled.

What a chain breaker. What a feeling of empowerment.

The process may be quite fragile. It might be missing people and components that were so very important to your life. But if you are still breathing, you can begin again.

"if you are still breathing, you can begin again"

9

Living in History

LUCILLE'S WISDOM

by Hazel Nurse

It all started several years ago when I received a phone call from my mother, inviting me to come to hear a speaker in Atlantic City.

Having just moved into another home a few months earlier, and bearing the responsibilities of a wife and working mom, I refused. She, on the other hand, insisted that I would miss listening to him tell America a few things. She said, "He has something on the ball."

Out of respect for her, I reluctantly got my pregnant self together, grabbed my seven-year-old son, and boarded a train to meet her. After his speech, we went and shook his hand, at the Atlantic City High School, in 1958.

Little did Mom know that a national holiday would be celebrated in honor of Dr. Martin Luther King, Jr.

POWER

by Hazel Nurse

With the welcoming of returning soldiers from Iraq, memories of wars past crowd my mind. One in particular really makes a point. A veteran of World War II, who was a paramedic, was driving his ambulance across a bridge in Düsseldorf, Germany. Little did he know that the bridge was mined. The explosives blew him into the water below. Although we were fighting the Germans, two German ladies pulled him to safety until help appeared. He was flown to Valley Forge hospital, were he remained for nine months.

"Don't underestimate the power of the human spirit."

He lived an extremely beautiful life to a ripe old age. Don't underestimate the power of the human spirit.

Snake Oil

by Joe Garrison

Most people still remember the days of the old-timer radio shows. There was no formatted radio back in those days. There were comedy and adventure and variety game shows. And there were very few discussions of the advertising practices in those days, especially advertising about medicine. What I mean is, there was a lot of medical quackery going on, but no critique of it.

One of the more famous commercials back in the late '40s was an ad for a dandruff shampoo. This shampoo was supposed to kill a germ that we found later was nonexistent. Around the 1950s, there was an ad for another very famous elixir. It was so popular there was a blues song written about it. This elixir consisted of ethyl alcohol and was habit forming. Hadacol was the name. It was a big craze. This medication became so popular. It was a cheap high, and a lot of people took it.

It was like another craze that happened back in the '30s called Ginger Jake. It was another alcoholic drink that was used as a medicine, mostly sold by the gangster element that was prevalent in those days. In contrast, these days, it's hard to put any kind of "snake oil" like these on the market, under the watchful eyes of the American Medical Association. However, some medicines that are advertised today I'd be wary of taking as well, because the side effects are worse than the ailments themselves.

BE ON THE ALERT

by Joe Garrison

Because of my disability, my mom was a little afraid of me playing with the sighted kids, and I stayed inside and watched TV. During the early days of TV there were not a lot of corporate sponsors, but they had public service announcements. This was at the beginning of the Cold War. Public service announcements were about civil defense. I remember two were scary, and they ran during children's programming times.

"This was the beginning of the cold war."

One commercial was about germ warfare and the other about a stealth bomb attack from another country. One began with a trumpet fanfare and horns blaring and people screaming. I was scared half to death to the point where I would have nightmares about these people running and screaming. I could understand about people being informed, but, to me, this was overkill!

Thank goodness they don't make commercials like that today! This also goes to show that when you're a child, you don't only learn about Mother Goose but you can also get a little taste of propaganda!

10

Romance

I Was the Original Fifty-Cent

by Brenda Bailey

I was not allowed to take company until I was sixteen, and throughout the days leading up to my birthday I had someone waiting in the wings, and his name was Buddy. He lived four doors down from me. We could only sit on my porch or his, walk to the corner store the long way, or attend school events, and then it was straight to home. Believe me, eyes and ears were everywhere—either his parents or mine.

After several months of talking, walking, and a few stolen kisses, Buddy gave me a shock. He told me he had been saving a year to buy the girl of his dreams a special gift and I was that girl—so he gave me a diamond ring. I said, "What! Are you crazy? My mother will kill me. Wow."

When I got into the house I called my best friend Linda and she screamed with excitement. I hid the ring and only wore it when I wanted to show off.

I had a job after school at HUP serving dinner trays to patients. One night while waiting for the bus to go home, I looked down to *"the stone was gone!"* admire the ring. I had just shown it to my co-workers before I left. To my horror, the stone was gone! What was I going to tell Buddy? As soon as I got in the house I called Linda. She said, "Buddy is going to have your head."

The next morning on the way to school Linda came up with a plan. We would go to the jewelry store on 40th and Market Streets and see how much another stone would cost. I explained to the jeweler how Buddy had saved for years to buy this ring and asked if he could replace the stone. I would pay on it every week from my paycheck, and he said he could replace it.

Linda was standing next to me holding my hand while I was waiting for the cost when the jeweler said, "Fifty cents." Linda fell to the floor laughing her head off, and I stood there in shock. When I came to my senses, I gave the jeweler fifty cents and he glued in the stone. It looked just like the original. He told me to leave the ring in the box for several days and then return the ring to Buddy, which I did.

When I married, Linda was my Maid of Honor, and she leaned over to me at my wedding and asked, "Is that a fifty-cent ring?" And when I had my first child, Linda said to name him "Fifty Cents." Of course I didn't. But for Linda, my nickname for years was "Fifty Cents."

Uptown Trash

by Hazel Nurse

Several years ago in the Atlantic City High School lunchroom, my friend Dorris introduced me to a young man who needed a date for his senior prom. At fourteen years of age, I wholeheartedly accepted his invitation, eagerly anticipating this new experience.

On prom night he appeared in a rented tuxedo with a corsage of red roses in hand. After attaching it to my older sister's full-length gown (borrowed from my older sister), I was excited. He ushered me to the back seat of a long jitney, chauffeured by a

"I was excited"

friend of his family. After a farewell from Mom and a lecture from Dad ensuring my return before midnight, we were off to an enjoyable evening.

Through the years we corresponded, and after one heated discussion I decided to end our friendship and called him "Uptown Trash." However, even after cutting him out of a photo, we were married eight years later.

A "Sadie Hawkins" Dance

by Joe Garrison

I was a junior in high school, and for the most part I always had to ask a girl to the dances. Because I wanted something to look forward to other than staying home and watching television, I went to just about every single dance. This one was different, because the girls asked the guys. I wasn't expecting any particular girl to ask me, but there were three girls who were very popular. I thought there was a chance one of these three girls would ask me. I wasn't very popular, but I was just hoping! Oh, I have to tell you the three girls' names: Ellie, Dinah, and Natalie. For about a month, I was really anticipating that maybe one of them would ask me. I thought very seriously about the possibility. I got to thinking about which one would ask me. Here's a hint—listen to the play on words. I thought Ellie may, Dinah might, but was sure Natalie would.

Did you catch the play on words?
Ellie ... May (like "Beverly Hillbillies'" Elly May Clampett.)
Dinah-mite ... (well, that spells dynamite.)
Natalie Wood ... (that's the name of a popular actress at the time.)

So, what I'm trying to say is, none of them asked me, and I ended up not going to the dance.
In fact, I remember that night it rained, and I stayed home. I ended up watching TV. The very same thing I didn't want to do. I really wanted to go to this dance, but I tried to take in stride.

MARRIAGE, A STATE OF MIND

by Joe Garrison

Debra was my favorite girl, and she reasoned, cared, and thought like a wife.

Four years ago I had a heart attack, and Debra was the one who told my sister and was by my side the whole time during my recovery.
I met her at work twenty years ago. We were first office mates and we became friends, and one thing led to another.

It was in '06 when we found out that we had been in love with each other all these years. Well, through the years we kept growing our friendship. I couldn't start my work day without saying good morning to her.

This relationship was based on true friendship. We became a sounding board for each other's problems and struggles.

I can write a whole book about Debra.

Because of who she was, her sweetness radiated through the whole agency where we worked. Everyone liked her, and the few people who didn't—I felt that they were just jealous of her.

This girl was the love of my life, and she passed away two years ago. She found out she had cancer in '08. Even though she is not here, I still feel as though she is here with me.

Believe it or not, sometimes when the wind is right, I still smell the fragrance of her hair. That's how much I loved her.

When I found out that she had passed away, I literally lost it. It took me six, seven months to accept the fact that she had passed. That's how much I loved her.

Debra was the sweetest girl I ever knew. If a person can find someone like that once in their life, they're fortunate; they have something good. True romantic love is the perfume of life.

"True romantic love is the perfume of life"

P.S. We had a special way of expressing our love to each other. We'd say Debra-Foreva, and that means she is mine forever.

11

Our Storytelling Group

The Best Time of My Life is Now
This Class
The Best Day of My Life Story

THE BEST TIME OF MY LIFE IS NOW

by Beatrice Newkirk

The best time now is being able to write about the best times of my life. To be able to remember things that were the best. Being able to talk about what is happening now. Doing things we could not have done in the past. Having a class to go to, like this writing class. To be able to put words down on paper and to afterwards read what you have written. Hearing stories from other people, you learn so much. Everyone has a story to tell. Some stories are good; some are sad.

"Everyone has a story to tell."

Some stories relate to other people. You may hear someone's stories and say that sounds like your story. The best time is now.

THIS CLASS

by Helen H. Lahr

I still remember that it was with some trepidation that I first joined this class last year. But ever since I stepped foot in this room, I've loved being part of this group.

"I feel alive and free."

The people are so nice, and when I'm here I don't get nervous sharing. Here, I feel alive and free.

When we write, we don't focus on our errors. Instead, we focus on learning from each other.

One test of how much I love this class was how I felt this summer. Because I take breaks from the Senior Center during the summer, I couldn't be in this class. When September finally came and I walked through the front door of the Senior Center again, it was this class that was on my mind.

I love being here.

I love you all.

THE BEST DAY OF MY LIFE STORY

by Robert Leung

My name is Yuk Tsun "Bobby" Leung. I call this story the best day of my life because after I joined this wonderful class in the Senior Center, I've met a lot of different people of all kinds and all colors. Because we are all human beings and we live in the same world, I come to the class each week and learn a lot.

I told my family and my children. They are all very, very happy for me. I look forward to each Thursday of every week. When I go to class we all have a good day, so that's why I call it "The Best Day of My Life."

> *"When I go to class we all have a good day."*